GUIDELINES FOR PREACHERS AND TEACHERS OF GOD'S WORD

BY DAVID AMOAH

Copyright © 2013 David Amoah

All rights reserved. No part of this publication may be produced, distributed, or transmitted in any form or by any means, including photocopying, recording, or other electronic or mechanical methods, without the prior written permission of the publisher, except in the case of brief quotations embodied in critical reviews and certain other noncommercial uses permitted by copyright law.

For permission requests, write to the publisher, addressed "Attention: Permissions Coordinator" at the email address below:

Life and Success Media Ltd

e-mail: info@lifeandsuccessmedia.com

www.lifeandsuccessmedia.com

Unless otherwise stated, all scripture quotations are taken from the Holy Bible, New King James Version. Quotations marked NKJV are taken from the HOLY BIBLE, NEW KING JAMES VERSION. Copyright © 1973, 1978, 1984 by International Bible Society. Used by permission of Hodder and Stoughton Ltd, a member of the Hodder Headline Plc Group. All rights reserved. "NKJV" is a registered trademark of International Bible Society. UK trademark number 1448790.

Quotations marked KJV are from the Holy Bible,

King James Version.

ISBN Number : 978-1-907402-76-0

Dedication

The Holy Spirit has been the best teacher I have ever had. He has brought me from nowhere to this wonderful place of being an author, and from nobody to somebody. My enthusiasm to preach and teach God's word and for me to be able to prepare these guidelines is all down to His leading. I am therefore happy to dedicate the work to Him to show my appreciation. Thank you God!

Contents

Foreword 7

Introduction 9

Preaching And Teaching 13

Preparation 21

The Holy Spirit is the best teacher 21
The importance of prayer 35
Other important points on preparation 41

Structure Of Preaching And Teaching 43

Theme and relevant messages..43
The main body of your message..45

Personal Conduct When Preaching Or Teaching 47

Presenting Your Message......................................49

Conveying your message clearly...50
Why be sensitive to the Holy Spirit when preaching or teaching? ...56
My personal experience as a young preacher 58

Other Important Points.......................................61

Preach Christ 65
Examples of preaching Christ..66

The true word will always provide better results 68
Personal testimony 72
Causing offense 73

Conclusion 79

Other Publications by Pastor David Amoah 83

Foreword

I highly recommend this training manual for all ministers, pastors and leaders to be, and to all those, even in post, in ministry today. This is a step-by-step guide to help you maximise your preaching or teaching ministry. As I have often said, 'It is always better to build a fence on top of a cliff than a hospital at the bottom'. Because, when preparation meets opportunity success is inevitable. This training manual will help prepare anyone who wants to succeed in their preaching or teaching ministry to make great impact, for it is training that turns trash into treasure. Please recommend it to all of your friends.

Bishop Michael Hutton-Wood
(President, Leaders Factory International, UK)

Introduction

I would first like to thank God who gave me the knowledge, courage and the material through the leading of the Holy Spirit to prepare for this 'manual'. I wrote this manual a few days after I wrote and preached a message entitled *What is in Your Hands?* This too is now being transformed into a book called *Your Future is in Your Hands*. My main point focuses on the fact that people do not value what they have in their hands or what God has given them, so they neglect what could have been a curtain-raiser in their lives. In the course of writing, I did not know I would write about myself. Like many others I did not know who I was, and what God had given me. A man of God has said to me on several occasions, 'You don't know who you are, and how valuable you are. You don't know what the Lord has made you'.

Also many people who listen to my preaching have advised me to teach people how to preach or teach. People even call the radio station, where I preach on a weekly basis, to tell me the same thing. Each time someone encourages me in this way a panic always rises within me and I say to myself: *Who am I to teach people how to preach or teach?*

Once again, I thank God for helping me to discover who I am and for what He has given me; the mandate to teach people how to preach and teach His (God's) word. On the fateful afternoon of Thursday 12 March 2009, I could not stop writing. I found myself responding to what I call the 'Macedonian Call' which means a call to teach people how to preach and teach.

Whether you are a minister, pastor, Sunday school teacher, group leader or an ordinary believer, if you want to be an effective communicator in your preaching and teaching, or if you want your preaching and teaching to be seasoned and attractive to your listeners, then I advise you to read and take these guidelines very seriously. It will be of great help to you, and is one of the ways in which you could improve and articulate the delivery of your message even if you are an ordinary believer witnessing to win souls for Christ. I am saying this because many preachers and teachers do not have the time to listen to other preachers and teachers and thereby learn from them. To become an effective preacher or teacher, it is important that you listen to those you think you can learn from. By doing so, it could help you to develop your style of delivery and improve the clarity of your message. Yes, we are all led by the Spirit, but it is also good to follow the example of those whose words and methods are inspired by the Spirit. Those who do this

Introduction

work need to be equipped very well. This book offers you guidelines, plus thoughts, to make you think about how to be a great preacher and teacher of God's word. I hope you will be blessed, and you will benefit from what I have said within these guidelines.

One of the major factors that inspired me to write these guidelines is that many people love to preach and teach, but have no idea how to do so. By this I mean how to preach properly, systematically, and in an orderly way. Even though it is difficult for me to say this I admit that I have listened to many preachers and teachers myself and can say that some people do not understand how to preach or teach. They are not experienced enough and therefore need to be taught. I don't doubt the fact that many are called to be preachers and teachers of God's word, but, I also believe that many need training. I once met a woman who, finding out that I was a pastor, asked me, 'Have you had training?' In fact, she even wanted to know when I had my training. She said, 'I am sorry to say it, but in my country so many people call themselves pastors, and yet they don't know how to preach because they have had no training.' I think she is right. Sometimes, when you listen to people preaching or teaching, you often wonder which part of the message is the beginning, middle or the end. This means that the message has no structure or format, which makes it very difficult for the listener to follow and absorb the content, or remember anything about the message afterwards. If God's word is to take root in the listener's conscience, then it must be delivered in a way which brings understanding and clarity.

I also believe that there are those who are aspiring or claiming to be preachers or teachers, but may not know or understand what a preacher or teachers is. It is important that these two roles are understood, as they form the basis of imparting and spreading God's word. These two roles are part of the ministerial gifts God gave to the Church.

Preaching And Teaching

Preaching and teaching, although closely related, are yet slightly different as they perform two quite different functions. Before I move on to discuss the guidelines in detail, I first want to show you the difference between preaching and teaching and how important these two callings are in the Kingdom of God.

PREACHING

Preaching is the proclamation of the good news of salvation through man to man, that is, man promulgating (spreading, proclaiming) the gospel to others to bring them to repentance and salvation and with the aim to bring or convert people to Christ.

The meaning of the word *gospel* is good news. The Gospel's teachings within the Bible instruct that Jesus Christ is the Son of God and that He is the saviour of the world. The Gospels teach how Jesus came to die, taking the punishment for the sins people of this world commit, and how He rose from the dead on the third day and ascended to heaven.

The Gospels teach us how Jesus will return and lead back, to his Father's kingdom, all those who believe in Him.

Examples of quotations to support my view above on preaching

"[1]In those days John the Baptist came *preaching* in the wilderness of Judea, [2]and saying, 'Repent, for the kingdom of heaven is at hand!'" (Matthew 3:1–2)

"[35]Then Jesus went about all the cities and villages, teaching in their synagogues, *preaching* the gospel of the kingdom, and healing every sickness and every disease among the people." (Matthew 9:35,)

"[15]And He said to them, 'Go into all the world and *preach* the gospel to every creature. [16]He who believes and is baptized will be saved; but he who does not believe will be condemned. [17]And these signs will follow those who believe: In My name they will cast out demons; they will speak with new tongues; [18]they will take up serpents; and if they drink anything deadly, it will by no means hurt them; they will lay hands on the sick, and they will recover.' [19]So then, after the Lord had spoken to them, He was received up into heaven, and sat down at the right hand of God. [20]And they went out and *preached* everywhere, the Lord working with *them* and confirming the word through the accompanying signs. Amen." (Mark 16:15–20)

"[18]The Spirit of the LORD is upon me, because He has anointed me to preach the gospel to the poor; He has sent me to heal the broken hearted, to proclaim liberty to the captives and recovery of sight to the blind, to set at liberty those who are oppressed." (Luke 4:18)

"So they departed and went through the towns, preaching the gospel and healing everywhere." (Luke 9:6)

"[30]Then Paul dwelt two whole years in his own rented house, and received all who came to him, [31]preaching the kingdom of God and teaching the things which concern the Lord Jesus Christ with all confidence, no one forbidding him." (Acts 28:30–31)

☞ TEACHING

Teaching is to impart the knowledge of God and Jesus Christ to the believer, in order to sustain him in his belief. The daily feeding of believers with the word of God will direct them about how to live a worthy life as a follower of Christ and also provide daily training for believers, which will help them to build a moral competence in Christ that is Christ-like.

Teaching is also about explaining the truth in the Scriptures, helping students to understand difficult passages and showing them how to apply God's word to their daily lives. A teacher will take a passage from God's word and interpret it with great clarity. The teacher will be able to engage his students by interacting with them through questions and contributions. This allows the teacher to connect with his students' or listeners' thoughts and ideas, and strengthen them by the wisdom and knowledge he imparts as their teacher.

Examples of quotations to support my view above on teaching

"'[19]Go therefore and make disciples of all the nations, baptizing them in the name of the Father and of the Son and of the Holy Spirit, [20]*teaching* them to observe all things that I have commanded you; and lo, I am with you always, *even* to the end of the age.' Amen." (Matthew 28:19–20, NKJV)

"A bishop then must be blameless, the husband of one wife, temperate, sober-minded, of good behaviour, hospitable, able to teach." (1 Timothy 3:2)

"These things command and teach."(1 Timothy 4:11)

"And those who have believing masters, let them not despise *them* because they are brethren, but rather serve *them* because those who are benefited are believers and beloved. Teach and exhort these things." (1 Timothy 6:2)

In summary, I would say that preaching brings the unbeliever to Christ while teaching instructs the regenerated how to live in Christ; teaching helps the born again Christian to grow in Christ.

Preachers and teachers are very important in God's Kingdom. Without them people will not hear the word and come to salvation. They also help people to live their lives according to the word of God. Paul said to the Roman Church (Romans 10: 14), 'How then shall they call on Him in whom they have not believed? And how shall they believe in Him of whom they have not heard? And how shall they hear without a preacher?'

In the Old Testament, Deuteronomy 25: 4 the scripture says that preachers and teachers must be well paid. This shows that they are very important in the body of Christ, despite the popularity of other ministerial gifts these days. This line of thinking is further endorsed by reading Timothy, illustrating how important it is to reward those who give their service to God by preaching and teaching. Therefore the work of those who preach and teach God's word should not be underestimated. 1 Timothy 5: 17–18 states: 'The elders who direct the affairs of the church well are worthy of **double honour,** especially those whose work is **preaching and teaching**.' For as the scripture says, 'Do not muzzle the ox while it is treading out the grain', and 'The worker deserves his wages.'

I come from a background where some ignorant people believe that ministers of the gospel, preachers and teachers of God's word and others that work in the context of doing their duty in God's Name, should not be paid. These people believe that God's work is a charitable vocation and those who are called to do this work must do so for free.

I can but call on the scriptures themselves to assert my belief that it is our duty to support those that do God's work. We cannot underestimate the importance of the work carried out by preachers and teachers of the word of God. The scriptures clearly state that preachers and teachers of God's word must be well looked after and well paid. Take for instance 1 Corinthians 9: 13–14, which states: 'Do you not know that those who minister the holy things eat *of the things* of the temple, and those who serve at the altar partake of *the offerings of* the altar? Even so the Lord has commanded that those who preach the gospel should live from the gospel.'

Let me again state what I have said many times when it comes to the matter of God's servants' remuneration: if other professionals are seen as deserving of a fee for work well done, are seen as deserving of a salary, payment or fee, then why not those whose work it is to lead man to salvation and godliness? Personally, I feel that this type of work should be even more richly rewarded.

Let me bring to my argument to a close with Paul, who entreats the Galatians to listen to him and remember to bless those who teach them the word of God, so that God might bless them. Paul says in Galatians 6: 6 'Let him who is taught the word share in all good things with him who teaches.'

As a minister of God's word myself, I can testify that many, many preachers and teachers only hear from those to whom they preach or teach when they are at their lowest and most distressed. Preachers and teachers thus spend many hours and expend freely and gladly energy and wisdom, helping to restore faith and counselling on how to face life's problems and challenges. They do not hear from people when things are going well. I do not think it is right, therefore, either morally or according to the scriptures to expect men and women tirelessly working in God's Name here on earth, to live by faith alone. Teachers and preachers of God's word should be richly rewarded for their work in God's name as the scriptures tell us.

Preparation

To prepare, get everything ready before starting. This is a good foundation for everything in this life, especially things that concern spirituality, such as preaching and teaching God's word. It is the key ingredient that makes any activity successful.

The Holy Spirit is the best teacher

In preparing your messages, as a pastor, teacher, or as an ordinary believer who would like to preach or teach God's word, I would like to give you some advice. Before you embark on any such mission, you must be taught how to do so. It is said that anybody who wants to lead must firstly be led. From my personal experience I advise that you first depend on the Holy Spirit for all your messages because He is the best teacher. He can teach you how and what to preach or teach. He knows what God holds for His people and also what people need to know. As it says in 1 Corinthians 2: 11: 'For who knows a person's thoughts except their own spirit within them? In the same way no one knows the thoughts of God except the Spirit of God.'

What a joy it is to preach or teach exactly what meets the needs of your listeners. Many parents will agree with me that it can be very disappointing to buy your child a birthday present only to be told that she or he does not like your present and therefore refuses to use it. If a preacher or teacher delivers the word of God and it alienates the listener, then the whole exercise is pointless. In order for a listener to learn, develop or grow, he or she must first grasp the essence of what the preacher or the teacher is saying. If the preacher or teacher is confused about what he or she is saying, then the listener will be even more confused. The point I am making is that clarity must be in the message. The Holy Spirit is the only 'tool' that brings clarity to our message, so you must rely on Him at all times. Solomon said (Proverbs 3: 5–6), 'Trust in the Lord with all your heart, And lean not on your own understanding; In all your ways acknowledge Him, And He shall direct your paths.' I believe that Solomon's message is very relevant here, in the current context.

Jesus reinforced this essential instruction; telling his disciples to depend on the Holy Spirit when He was about to send them out to preach the gospel. In Luke 12: 12 we are told that Jesus said, 'For the Holy Spirit will teach you in that very hour what you ought to say.' In John 14: 26 we learn also that Jesus said: 'The Counsellor, the Holy

Spirit, whom the Father will send in my name, will teach you all things and will remind you of everything I have said to you.' The Holy Spirit is the reason why the ordinary men of Galilee turned into apostles, who made history by turning the world upside down with the gospel. They preached and taught the word of God with power because they depended on the Holy Spirit, just as Jesus Christ had promised them in Acts 1: 8: 'But you shall receive power when the Holy Spirit has come upon you; and you shall be witnesses to Me in Jerusalem, and in all Judea and Samaria, and to the end of the earth.'

In his letter to the Corinthian Church (2 Corinthians 3: 5–6) Paul wrote, 'Not that we are sufficient of ourselves to think of anything as being from ourselves, but our sufficiency is from God, who also made us sufficient as ministers of the new covenant, not of the letter but of the Spirit; for the letter kills, but the Spirit gives life.'

I am a living testimony and the embodiment of what I advocate. Since giving my life to Christ, and from the very beginning of my ministry, the Holy Spirit has helped me and led me to preach and teach effectively. Because I depend on Him, He also gives me the desire to preach and teach; something which I take great pleasure in doing. I promise you—if you too depend on Him—He will not let you down.

Jesus' messages made a great difference because He had the backing of the Holy Spirit. The Holy Spirit gave Jesus the strength and authority to deliver His message and command the attention of His followers and detractors alike. Matthew 7: 28–29 states, 'When Jesus had finished saying these things, the crowds were amazed at his teaching because He taught as one who had authority, and not as their teachers of the law.' The Holy Spirit will bring conviction to your listeners if you depend on Him when you preach or teach. There are many preachers and teachers of God's word today as it was in the days of Jesus Christ, but just as Jesus' messages made a difference from that of the teachers of the law and the Pharisees, you can also make a difference in your preaching and teaching when you depend on the Holy Spirit.

As a preacher and teacher, I can testify how encouraging it is to know that my preaching or teaching has spoken directly to someone's situation. The essence of teaching and preaching is to address the spiritual needs of your congregation using the word of God in an informed and profound way. You must have conviction and authority in what you are saying. If you are not well prepared or do not have confidence in what you are saying, then you are in danger of misrepresenting God's message and misleading people. Plus, they will see through the weakness of your message and will not be convinced of your sincerity. In other words, if you are ill-prepared, then you will fail at two levels; you will fail as a preacher or a teacher and you will also fail your congregation. The only way to do this work is by relying on the strength and authority of the Holy Spirit. Paul told the Corinthian Church (1 Corinthians 2: 4–5): 'And my speech and my preaching were not with persuasive words of human wisdom, but in demonstration of the Spirit and of power, that your faith should not be in the wisdom of men but in the power of God.' Many people today have their faith in the wisdom of men instead of Christ so no wonder many of them have fallen away, because the messages they receive are the persuasive words of human wisdom, not messages inspired by the Holy Spirit.

Paul further states in 1 Corinthians 2: 11–12: 'For what man knows the things of a man except the spirit of the man which is in him? Even so, no one knows the things of God except the Spirit of God. Now we have received, not the spirit of the world, but the Spirit who is from God, that we might know the things that have been freely given to us by God.'

And in 1 Corinthians 2: 14: 'The man without the Spirit does not accept the things that come from the Spirit of God, for they are foolishness to him, and he cannot understand them, because they are spiritually discerned.'

As a preacher and teacher of God's word, the Holy Spirit is the best teacher I have ever had. Personally, I always depend on God when it comes to what to preach or teach. He has never disappointed me. Many times I have marvelled at how He directs me to quotations and how He points out to me things to say during my preparations, and even while I am preaching or teaching.

Again, Paul wrote to the Thessalonians (1 Thessalonians 1: 4–5) and told them: 'For we know, brothers loved by God, that he has chosen you, because our gospel came to you not simply with words, but also with power, with the Holy Spirit and with deep conviction.' So, I say, learn to depend on the Holy Spirit for guidance about what to preach or teach. Be taught by him and you can also preach and teach effectively. It should also be borne in mind that one of the ways the devil deprives people from listening to the word of God is by causing them to sleep when the word is been preached, but let me assure you of this, if your message is backed up by the Holy Spirit no one will sleep or want you to stop, as on some occasions listeners are apt to do.

Be well prepared

To misinterpret text in the Bible is to abuse it. Therefore, as a teacher or as a preacher you should not quote text until you yourself fully understand its message. When you are interpreting a text, you are probing into it and looking closely at the words, passages and phrases so that you are able to preach or teach it with clarity to your listeners. Many people, Christians, especially some church leaders, think preaching or teaching is their opportunity to gain popularity, thus they fight their way to the pulpit whether they are well prepared or not.

My advice on this matter is that it is better to refuse to preach or teach when you are not well prepared. It is better to stay away from the pulpit than to preach badly or teach ineffectively because you are not well prepared.

Most importantly, the preacher must always have something solid to say when he is behind the pulpit. The preacher must not say things such as, "I don't know what to say", because your listeners are always ready to receive something from you and trust in your knowledge.

In spite of the increased importance placed on effective communication these days, many preachers and teachers continue to struggle with this skill and are unable to communicate successfully. That is, they fail to preach or to teach effectively. *Note that to become a good communicator in the context of being an effective preacher or teacher takes hard work; preparation must be paramount in the life of every preacher or teacher of God's word. The effective preacher or teacher must spend time in preparation of his message. Many people fail in life and in examinations because of their lack of preparation. In the same way, many people fail or struggle during preaching or teaching or when they are behind the pulpit because they are not adequately prepared. If you want to deliver a good and convincing message you must be well prepared.* After seeking the help and direction of the Holy Spirit, you must execute the practical side of preparation. There is an organising process when it comes to preparedness and it involves action. Do not sit down and think the Holy Spirit will tell you what to say. You still have to get into the process of preparing your message well. This should include finding examples that bring out the essence of your message; looking for relevant and supporting scriptures which underpin your themes; and making sure that everything you say will add value to your message. To be well prepared is to be well informed. I remember a man who failed totally behind the pulpit whilst preaching. Talking to him later I discovered that he did not prepare at all; he thought he knew his topic very well and therefore there was no need for any more preparation. If Jesus Christ, the head of the Church spent thirty years to prepare for His three years of ministry, why should not you and I prepare equally thoroughly for our ministry?

Prayer is a crucial tool in the process of preparation, delivery, conviction, and sustenance. Therefore pray before, and after, your messages. Commit yourself to God. Ask the Holy Spirit to use you to bless your listeners and pray against any opposing forces or spirits that will try to hinder or suppress your message.

Paul asked the Colossians to pray for him knowing that prayers help preachers and teachers of God's word. In Colossians 4: 3–4, it is written: 'And pray for us, too, that God may open a door for our message, so that we may proclaim the mystery of Christ, for which I am in chains. Pray that I may proclaim it clearly, as I should.' As a preacher and teacher myself I can boldly say, without any regret, that sadly not all listeners are genuinely or truly seeking God's word. Many of them are 'killers' and so you need God's protection against such people.

I once watched an Evangelist Bonnke crusade DVD in the Northern region of Ghana. During the crusade the camera caught someone in the crowd lifting a chicken. What do you think he was doing? I believe that person was trying to use evil spirits to disrupt the service, but, thank God, the Holy Spirit was on the move, so everything proceeded perfectly.

Always be up-to-date and current

Within the context of these guidelines, I have a precise definition of the term 'be updated'. Some preachers and teachers make no effort to update their knowledge and understanding. They use irrelevant or out-of-date information to preach or teach. This is not good practice. So in the process of preparation:

- Acquire knowledge in order to be able to pass knowledge to others. Spend time studying the Bible. There is a strong possibility that you could lead your listeners astray if you don't study properly. Describing the Pharisees to his disciples Jesus said (Matthew 15: 14): 'Let them alone. They are blind leaders of the blind. And if the blind leads the blind, both will fall into a ditch.'

- Be very familiar with what you are preaching or teaching. That is to say, study your message very well. Learn everything you must know about your chosen topic. Paul, advising his son in Christ, the young pastor Timothy, said to him (2 Timothy 2: 15): 'Be diligent to present yourself approved to God, a worker who does not need to be ashamed, rightly dividing the word of truth.'

I believe that these words were written to Timothy but also for all believers in that text. I also believe that these words are relevant to preachers and teachers of God's word, as it advises them to study their messages well in order not to disgrace themselves before an audience.

Thank God for Martin Luther. The time of the lone fish in the pond is over. The time of only one Bible which the minister alone read and then preached is over. Wisdom has abounded, as Daniel (12: 4) predicted: 'But you, Daniel, shut up the words, and seal the book until the time of the end; many shall run to and fro, and knowledge shall increase.'

Preachers and teachers, some of your listeners could be like the people of Berea in Paul's day. In Acts 17: 11 it says, 'Now the Bereans were of more noble character than the Thessalonians, for they received the message with great eagerness and examined the scriptures every day to see if what Paul said was true.'

At a later date, your listeners might want to study what you have said, only to find out that your information is wrong. So be careful not to disgrace yourself before them. Give your listeners accurate and up-to-date information. Arm yourself with the gift of truth and knowledge. Be led by the Spirit, because the currency of accuracy is powerful and transformative. It will have an impact on your listeners. It will reach the depths of their souls and bless them. It will bring a new understanding to them and will add clarity to your message.

When I was at Bible school, there were students there who were studying only to acquire knowledge; they had no intention of becoming pastors or ministers. In fact there were even more of these students than the full-time ones, among whom, some were already ministers. There will be times when you will have such people in your audience, so it is important that you study your message thoroughly. You should become very familiar with what you are saying in order to be able to persuade your listeners. During my time at Bible school, sometimes, the students would be sent to practise preaching in churches on Sundays. Some of the members at these churches were retired apostles and pastors and so you can imagine how knowledgeable these people were. You can imagine too how nerve-wracking it could be if you were the preacher or teacher. But, thank God, with the help of the Holy Spirit and proper preparation, we were able to do our best. I remember one night after I had preached about ten people came forward to be prayed for. My principal told me later that this was not a common occurrence. I believe that if you know the word, when you study your message thoroughly with the Holy Spirit's support, you will become a powerful preacher or teacher.

In 1 Corinthians 2: 4–5, Paul said: 'My message and my preaching were not with wise and persuasive words, but with a demonstration of the Spirit's power. So that your faith might not rest on men's wisdom, but on God's power.'

Know the word as a preacher or teacher

There are many believers who do not know how to witness or preach the word of God because they do not know the Bible. When you are knowledgeable in the word, you will be able to defend your faith when, or wherever, the need arises. When you are well prepared and knowledgeable in the word, it will help you to become a good preacher or teacher. These two factors will equip you to teach others effectively. It is impossible to teach others if you are not well versed in the knowledge you are going to impart. In others words, if you are limited in your understanding of your material, then you could be dismissed as one who is not equipped to deliver God's word. God needs representatives who will deliver His message with authority. For instance, a preacher who has Muslim background was invited to our church to teach us how we, as Christians, should approach Muslims confidently with the gospel of Christ. Unfortunately, during his teaching we discovered that he was not good enough; he was limited in his knowledge and therefore was unable to answer many of the questions we presented to him and we had to close the meeting earlier.

In 1 Timothy 4: 13–16, Paul said:

> 'Until I come, devote yourself to the public reading of scripture, to preaching and to teaching. Do not neglect your gift, which was given you through a prophetic message when the body of elders laid their hands on you. Be diligent in these matters; give yourself wholly to them, so that everyone may see your progress. Watch your life and doctrine closely. Persevere in them, because if you do you will save yourself and your hearers.'

He also said, in 2 Timothy 2: 1–2:

> 'You therefore, my son, be strong in the grace that is in Christ Jesus. And the things that you have heard from me among many witnesses, commit these to faithful men who will be able to teach others also.'

In Titus 1: 9 Paul said to the overseers that he must 'hold firmly to the trustworthy message as it has been taught, so that he can encourage others by sound doctrine and refute those who oppose it'.

In 1 Peter 3: 15, Peter said, 'But sanctify the Lord God in your hearts, and always *be* ready to *give* a defence to everyone who asks you a reason for the hope that is in you, with meekness and fear.'

Even though it is obvious that all the quotations above apply to all believers, I also see them as sound advice for preachers and teachers.

The importance of prayer

As a preacher or teacher of God's word, praying before and after preaching should be your priority. You must be aware as you are preaching and teaching that maybe not all of your listeners will be happy to see people being saved or delivered. These kinds of people will fight or oppose you, either spiritually or physically. They might even interrupt you. How many times have men of God been confronted by enemies and evil spirits when preaching or teaching? Even Jesus Christ was confronted by men and evil spirits during his time of preaching and teaching. The Pharisees hypocritically presented themselves at all Jesus' meetings for that purpose. The good news is that no matter what form they came in, Jesus defeated them with His words through the power of the Holy Spirit because He was always prepared in prayer.

Please note that you don't necessarily become an effective preacher simply because you are highly educated or eloquent. Effective preaching is when the heart is touched and the transformation leads people into repentance. It also makes a difference through the anointing of the Holy Spirit. In other words, it is your anointed message.

E. M. Bounds said:

> 'What the Church needs today is not more machinery/equipment or better, not new organizations or more and novel methods, but men whom the Holy Ghost can use—men of prayer, men mighty in prayer. The Holy Ghost does not flow through methods, but through men. He does not come on machinery, but on men. He does not anoint plans, but men—men of prayer.'

He went on to say:

> 'The real sermon is made in the closet. The man— God's man— is made in the closet. His life and his profoundest convictions were born in his secret communion with God. The burdened and tearful agony of his spirit, his weightiest and sweetest messages were got when alone with God. Prayer

makes the man; prayer makes the preacher; prayer makes the pastor.'

(Source: http://christian-quotes.ochristian.com/E.M.Bounds-Quotes/page-4.shtml)

Jesus made so much difference with his own preaching and teaching of his word because He was anointed; He spent time in prayer to prepare for his task ahead. Luke 4: 18–19 states:

'The Spirit of the Lord is upon Me, because He has anointed Me to preach the gospel to the poor; He has sent Me to heal the broken-hearted, To proclaim liberty to the captives and recovery of sight to the blind, To set at liberty those who are oppressed; To proclaim the acceptable year of the Lord.'

Jesus Christ understood the power of prayer. The Bible says Jesus often withdrew to quiet, solitary places to pray as told in Luke 5: 15–17:

'However, the report went around concerning Him all the more; and great multitudes came together to hear, and to be healed by Him of their infirmities. So He Himself often withdrew into the wilderness and prayed. Now it happened on a certain day, as He was teaching that there were Pharisees and teachers of the law sitting by, who had come out of every town of Galilee, Judea, and Jerusalem. And the power of the Lord was present to heal them'.

If Jesus had to spend time in prayer for strength to do His work, we humans need to do the same, if not more. As the apostles began their task, Jesus commissioned them with prayer as we learn in Acts 1:12–14:

'Then they returned to Jerusalem from the mount called Olivet, which is near Jerusalem, a Sabbath day's journey. And when they had entered, they went up into the upper room where they were staying: Peter, James, John, and Andrew; Philip and Thomas; Bartholomew and Matthew; James, the son of Alphaeus and Simon the Zealot; and Judas the son of James. These all continued with one accord in prayer and supplication, with the women and Mary the mother of Jesus, and with His brothers.'

And in Acts 2:41–42:

'Then those who gladly received his word were baptized; and that day about three thousand souls were added to them. And they continued steadfastly in the apostles' doctrine and fellowship, in the breaking of bread, and in prayers.'

Acts 2:47 reads: '…. praising God and having favour with all the people. And the Lord added to the church daily those who were being saved.'

While in Acts 4:31 we learn: 'And when they had prayed, the place where they were assembled together was shaken; and they were all filled with the Holy Spirit, and they spoke the word of God with boldness.'

To be an effective preacher or teacher of God's word you must also be prayerful for God will always respond to the prayers of His people who wait upon Him in prayer in their preparation to preach or teach.

In Ephesians 6:19–20 Paul asked for prayers:

> 'Pray also for me, that whenever I speak, words may be given me so that I will fearlessly make known the mystery of the gospel, for which I am an ambassador in chains. Pray that I may declare it fearlessly, as I should.'

Paul asked for prayers in Colossians 4:2–4:

> 'Devote yourselves to prayer, being watchful and thankful. And pray for us, too, that God may open a door for our message, so that we may proclaim the mystery of Christ, for which I am in chains. Pray that I may proclaim it clearly, as I should.'

And again in 2 Thessalonians 3:1–3:

> 'As for other matters, brothers and sisters, pray for us that the message of the Lord may spread rapidly and be honoured, just as it was with you. And pray that we may be delivered from wicked and evil people, for not everyone has faith. But the Lord is faithful, and he will strengthen you and protect you from the evil one.'

The author of the book of Hebrews also asked for prayers (13:18–19):

> 'Pray for us. We are sure that we have a clear conscience and desire to live honourably in every way. I particularly urge you to pray so that I may be restored to you soon.'

Other important points on preparation

- In most cases you can prepare messages after you have been given topics or an invitation. You are advised not always to wait until you are given an opportunity to preach or teach before you prepare. Constantly write or prepare messages and make it a positive habit. Do so as you read the Bible every day. You will eventually work out that this is a good thing to do when you preach or teach at a prayer day, Sunday sermon or Bible study class.

- For your study materials, use a range of different Bible translations and a good selection of Bible dictionaries. These can be very effective tools which can help you to improve accuracy and clarity.

- It is also effective to use notes during preaching or teaching. They can act as a guide to keep you systematically on track. Preachers like a pastor I knew at Penygroes in South Wales and T. D. Jakes, deliver their sermons very well without the aid of notes. Thank God for them, but the advice given here is that the ability to improvise is not something that everyone is blessed with.

Know your audience

As you prepare to preach or teach, or to honour an invitation to do either, it is very useful to know your audience. This will definitely help you in your preparation. Also the cultural and educational levels of the learners, whether with great strength of faith, believers or unbelievers, church members or non-church members, it is important for you to know as much about them as possible. As a preacher or teacher, having first-hand knowledge of the people you are preaching to or teaching will help you deliver a more relevant message. Otherwise, you might deliver a message that is not relevant to your listeners.

Structure Of Preaching And Teaching

The message you are preaching or teaching must be well structured. The following is a guideline on how to do this.

Theme and relevant messages

Don't confuse your congregation with multiple ideas; have a theme or a topic for all your messages. Be specific about your subject.

You don't give a theme a name for the sake of it; choose one that is relevant and one that will speak to your listeners. A relevant message will also mean that the preaching or teaching must be in the spirit of the occasion. For example, when you are asked to preach or teach at a prayer meeting, you must concentrate on what you have been asked to speak about. A typical example of what I am talking about here is, for example, when someone is asked to begin or end a meeting or service with prayer but instead they use this time to preach. Alternatively, another may pray but not focus on the things they were asked to pray for.

Theme/key quotation, also known as the foundation scripture

You need a theme, key quotations or a foundation scripture that go with your theme; you must then make sure that the quotations you have selected to go with your theme 1are relevant; that you haven't chosen a theme and quotations but then go on to talk about something else completely different. Stick to your theme and preach about your main quotation, even though you may have other supporting quotations. Many preachers and teachers will give a theme and quotation but preach or teach something different. What is even worse is when a preacher or teacher gives incorrect quotations, especially if listeners then turn to a quotation only to find that it is wrong. A preacher I listened to once gave three consecutive incorrect quotations. This is inexcusable in an era where access to knowledge abounds. Mistakes like this will switch off your audience or listeners.

Introduce the reason for your message or theme

This is when you explain to your audience what you are going to tell them about. In other words, you are introducing your listeners to your subject or telling your audience what they should expect. The readiness of your listeners very much depends on your introduction. Your message should whet the audience's appetite. Make it appealing to them, but avoid the temptation of spending too much time on the introduction. The introduction can be given before or after you have introduced your foundation scripture or theme and main quotation. The order in which this is delivered very much depends on the preacher or the teacher's personal style.

The main body of your message

Tell your listeners about your message (what you are telling them about). Here are some aspects of that:

- **Exegesis:** The background of what you are telling them, which is based on the theme and quotation and will include who the author of your quotation is, what it is for and why it is being introduced.

- **Hermeneutics:** Relate what you have read from the Bible to the present circumstances of your audience or listeners. Failure to connect the Bible with your audience's present circumstances will have a detrimental impact. You can add personal testimonies or give some examples. Maybe even share some jokes that will keep your listeners alert and on track with you. While doing all these things, make sure you do not lose concentration on the main thrust of your message, as many often do.

- **Conclusion:** Summarise everything you have said so far in your preaching or teaching. Then indicate to your listeners that your message is coming to an end. A good structured message or lesson always makes it easy for the listener to follow. You may or may not know that some preachers or teachers of the gospel hardly include an introduction, a body or a conclusion in their delivery. This is not the example to follow. To end their message on a good note or to conclude their message, some preachers and teachers uses phrases such as 'in conclusion', 'finally', 'as I bring my message to a close' or 'to end my message'. Closing in this way alerts your listeners to the fact that you are about to finish your message, and gives them the opportunity to prepare themselves mentally to end the message with you.

Personal Conduct When Preaching Or Teaching

Maintain good posture when preaching or teaching

Posture in preaching or teaching is very important; it is similar to someone leading praise and worship. The way you conduct yourself and your style can have a huge effect on your listeners. Some people's appearance and approach to preaching, teaching, or leading praise and worship can be very boring. A poor style of delivering your message means that the audience or listeners gain little in the way of motivation or inspiration. It is essential to approach the pulpit with energy and empathy, here are some guidelines.

Present your message with enthusiasm

Make it lively. Some begin their preaching with a song, others shout, 'Hallelujah, Praise God, and clap for Jesus' and so on. But don't forget that too much of this can become jargon and could switch off your listeners.

Respect and connect with your listeners or audience

Approach the pulpit with dignity for God and your listeners. Treat your listeners with respect. Respect them, because they took the time to come to the service; for they are hungry for the word of God. Some of these people may only have the opportunity to hear the word once a week. Don't waste that precious time. Knowing all of this requires that you, as a preacher or teacher, have a responsibility to show your listeners that you value them.

Look at your listeners. Smile at them. Keep them awake. All of these actions are crucial if you want them to maintain contact and engage and remain interested in what you have to say.

Presenting
Your Message

Present your message with boldness and enthusiasm, and be passionate in preaching or teaching. My principal, Bryn Thomas of the Apostolic School of Ministry always says, 'Present your message as a person who represents God; as a messenger of God.' In other words you are there not only to preach or teach to your listeners, but also to prove to them that you are passionate about what you are preaching or teaching.

What I am going to tell you next I share with you to the glory of God and not in order to boast: I am passionate when presenting my messages and have been told so many times. Sometimes people phone me when I am live on the radio and say that the Bible comes alive for them whenever they hear me preach. Others say that for them I present the word of God like a reporter or commentator, almost as if I am reporting live from an actual incident; I have been told by several people who have heard me preach that they feel I am actually present at the scene where the story happened. My listeners in Church become more joyful when they listen to me; I see it in their faces sometimes. This is good, for it does boost my morale and helps me to preach and teach better. Most of all it means that I am doing my work of spreading God's word well.

Conveying your message clearly

If you want to be sure your preaching or teaching is being received correctly, it is important that you know what your message is! Note that whatever it is you may be trying to tell your listeners your tone of voice, body language and choice of words will all convey what sort of person you are.

Your audience or listeners will get a strong sense of how you feel about your message; either you live by what you are telling them or you are just saying what you yourself don't or will not practice. It has to be clear through your message what you want your listener to do and how you want him or her to feel. As a result, this helps you to ensure that the right message is being conveyed. This is why sharing personal testimonies in preaching and teaching helps.

- Never preach or teach a topic, or use words and quotations you don't understand if you are uncomfortable or unfamiliar with them. It will be extremely difficult for anyone's words to flow in such circumstances. There are also those who use words and topics they have heard of, or seen somewhere, though they may not be fluent in delivering them. Sometimes it is a good idea to borrow words and phrases you have heard other people, preachers or teachers use, for it may well improve your own preaching and teaching skills, but use them with caution, and only when you comfortable with them.

- Be specific, and precise, and stick to your theme. By this I mean——stay on track—overcome the temptation to talk about everything you know from the Bible and stick to your theme. Some people think showing their knowledge of the Bible will impress their listeners and prove that they are good at what they do. These people will say anything that comes into their mind in one preaching or teaching session. This is why I recommend that notes are helpful.

- Be time-conscious. For even though we are being used by the Holy Spirit, you must yet be conscious about the time you have been given to preach or teach. Try as hard as you can to stick to your time-slot, and if you can't complete the message, you can always continue another time. Do not say, as I have heard many others announce, 'I am been used by the Holy Spirit so I can't stop', just because you don't feel like finishing. Finish when you are supposed to, and return another time to continue if necessary.

- Speak with clarity. A message is only successful when both the sender and the receiver perceive it in the same way. Your listeners must understand your message, just as you understand it yourself. Ensure that your message is well understood. This is paramount, and it is a key to your progress. To achieve this you must understand three things: first what your message means, second what the circumstance of the audience you are sending it to are, and third, how you expect the audience to perceive the message.

As Paul said in 1 Corinthians 14:6:

> 'Now, brothers, if I come to you and speak in tongues, what good will it be to you, unless I bring you some revelation or knowledge or prophecy or word of instruction?'

Even in the case of lifeless things that make sounds, such as the flute or harp, how will anyone know what tune is being played unless there is a distinction in the notes? Again, if the trumpet does not sound a clear call who will get ready for battle? So it is with you and your audience or listeners. Unless you speak intelligible words with your tongue, how will anyone understand what you are saying? You will just be speaking into the air. There are so many languages in the world, and none of them is insignificant.

In 1 Corinthians 14:18–19 Paul says:

> 'I thank my God I speak with tongues more than you all; yet in the church I would rather speak five words with my understanding, that I may teach others also, than ten thousand words in a tongue.'

Even though the quotation above refers to speaking in tongues it is still relevant advice to preachers and teachers of God's word. It explains that it is important to speak clearly at a level your listeners will understand. If you do not aim your message at your audience or listener's level they will not benefit from your preaching and they, and you, will be wasting time.

I was in the process of writing this manual when, one morning, the Lord spoke to me while I was praying. This manual is not only for those who preach from the pulpit, it should also be for those people who would like to witness too. The Lord explained that while many people love to witness to others or do evangelistic work, the reason why souls are not won over for Christ is because they speak without clarity. People don't clearly receive the message they are being told. Unless your listeners or audience understands you clearly, the message you are conveying will not be convincing and they will not be able to respond or repent. So, I say, from any level that you preach, teach or witness to others; if you want your message to be fruitful make sure that your message is clear. You must ensure your listener understands fully what you are telling him and accepts what you are telling him.

As a Ghanaian born and bred in Ghana who is now living in the United Kingdom, I know how to preach to an African audience and, to be more precise, Ghanaians. I also know how to preach to people in the UK. This is very important, because some words and analogies I use to preach to Ghanaians will not be relevant to my UK-based brethren. Even at my local church where we have services both in English and Ghanaian (Twi) languages, I can use the same Bible quotation for both services but the interpretation will differ, because my audiences are different.

Why be precise?

Some preachers would like to recite everything they know from the Bible in one go, as I mentioned earlier. What are they trying to prove? Is it that they want to show how much they know? As a preacher myself, I know that there is a temptation to say too much. Please take my advice—don't say everything in one sermon. This does not make you a good preacher but an inexperienced one. After all, you have a maximum of forty-five minutes to one hour to preach. After long periods, people become tired, fed up, and lose their concentration and they will switch off from anything further you say. Some preachers, as I have already warned, will plead, 'But I am being used by the Holy Spirit so I cannot stop'. No! You can. Just discipline yourself. Remember what Paul said (1 Corinthians 14:32) about prophets, 'The spirits of prophets are subject to the control of prophets.' What Paul means by this is that although you are being used by the Holy Spirit, you still have the control to stop whenever you want. Unlike demonic spirits that control a man without his will, the Holy Spirit is subject to you the preacher or teacher and will obey anything you want Him to do even though He is directing you.

Why present the gospel in a culturally relevant way?

Because when you present the gospel in a culturally relevant way you are speaking the language your listeners will understand.

a. Use a quotation and explanation that relates to your listeners' situation. You will be able to do exactly this as you wait on God in prayer. Then, you must follow the direction of the Holy Spirit. For His listeners to understand him fully, Jesus sometimes used parables to convey His messages (using brief human-based stories or things to convey spiritual truth) such as, 'The kingdom of heaven is like …'

b. Knowing what message you are bringing and why. Circumstances and the time or the season can be a contributing factor to this.

Why be sensitive to the Holy Spirit when preaching or teaching?

As you preach and teach and are sensitive to the Holy Spirit, He will help you with wisdom and guide you as to what to say and what not to say. Many preachers and teachers, because of their lack of sensitivity to the Holy Spirit, do not know when the Spirit is finished with them. When you are sensitive to the Holy Spirit you will know when to end your message.

Acts 16: 6–10 is a fitting quotation to use in relation to being sensitive to the Holy Spirit:

> 'Now when they had gone through Phrygia and the region of Galatia, they were forbidden by the Holy Spirit to preach the word in Asia. After they had come to Mysia, they tried to go into Bithynia, but the Spirit did not permit them. So passing

by Mysia, they came down to Troas. And a vision appeared to Paul in the night. A man of Macedonia stood and pleaded with him, saying, "Come over to Macedonia and help us." Now after he had seen the vision, immediately we sought to go to Macedonia, concluding that the Lord had called us to preach the gospel to them.'

From the quotation above it is clear that the Holy Spirit had different plans to those Paul and his companion had about when and where they should preach, despite them being on a missionary trip.

Being sensitive will also mean He can give you messages when you least expect it. This can happen through conversations, things you see and hear, when you are listening to other preachers and when you are meditating on God's word.

Never use quotations and statements that cannot be supported in the Bible. Some preachers often use statements and quotations they've heard from other people, even though they are not sure if these statements and quotations are in the Bible. Some of your listeners might want to learn more afterwards, so ensuring that quotes or statements are attributable is good practice for every student. Paul recommended the same about the Berean Church when he stated in Acts 17:11:

> 'Now the Bereans were of more noble character than the Thessalonians, for they received the message with great eagerness and examined the scriptures every day to see if what Paul said was true.'

My personal experience as a young preacher

As mentioned earlier, I have had a love for preaching since day one after I was Born Again. This led to a wonderful experience that I will never forget. In those early days I loved to preach to travellers, because I found that a journey is one of the easiest places, one of the most reliable situations, during which you can get people to pay attention and listen to the word of God. So when I travelled long distances, I would use what we in Ghana call the 'passenger car'. Any time I travelled I would normally use the large passenger car because it took more passengers. I would make directly for either the back seat or sit on the front seat. As soon as the driver moved off I would stand up, whilst the vehicle was moving, and begin to preach. One day travelling from Konongo to Kumasi in the Ashanti Region, I had just finished preaching when I sensed that my message had had a great impact on many of the passengers. It affected them so much that they started to give me offerings, even though I had not asked for any. At the end of the journey in Kumasi, one old man, who was in the same vehicle, came to me and said, 'Well done young man for the message. That was a good message. Could you give me the Bible quotation that you used, so that when I go home I can also read it?' I was a young believer, with little experience and even less knowledge in God's word, so I said something about Noah and the Flood story. But the statement I had used in my message was not from the Bible. Rather, it was something I had heard said many times since I was young. I looked in the book of Genesis, flipping from page to page without finding the quote. The old man seeing that I could not find the quote, and to my relief, pulled out a piece of paper and a pen on which he wrote his address, 'Take it,' he said, 'any time you find that quotation, post it to me.' He then offered me some more money and said you can buy stamp with it.

I have not been able to write to this man to this day because the story I used is not in the Bible. It is something I heard from someone and then repeated it because I was young in the Lord. Surprisingly, while writing this book of guidelines, I was listening to a local Ghanaian radio station one day when I heard a minister preaching who made use of the exact same story I so regretted using all those years ago. This is because the story is one that Ghanaians recite a lot, even though it is not in the Bible. This is not good practise and you should not try to pass of popular stories as biblical truth. Never use statements or quotations while preaching or teaching just because you have heard someone else using them. Use it because it is in the Bible.

Other Important Points

Preach the word of God

Never use the pulpit for your own purposes. It is there for you to carry out God's purpose, or to deliver God's word to his children who have given up their time to listen to you. The pulpit is not a right but a privilege. Paul thanks Christ Jesus our Lord for His faith in him when He committed the gospel to his trust.

Feeling that God's faith in him was undeserved Paul says in 1Timothy 1: 11–13:

> 'According to the glorious gospel of the blessed God which was committed to my trust. And I thank Christ Jesus our Lord who has enabled me, because He counted me faithful, putting me into the ministry, although I was formerly a blasphemer, a persecutor, and an insolent man; but I obtained mercy because I did it ignorantly in unbelief.'

In Ephesians 3: 7 the apostle explains, 'I became a servant of this gospel by the gift of God's grace, given me, through the working of His power.' By this, Paul means the opportunity to become a servant of God. Serving God by preaching and teaching the gospel is by the grace of God. Therefore when you step into the pulpit do your work humbly and wholeheartedly, like a servant who is serving his master.

It is unfortunate that some preachers use the pulpit to insult others or to talk about a dispute between themselves and others. There are also those who use the pulpit to tell the congregation how much better he is in relation to the leader or even the pastor he works under. Hear me and let this sink into your total being whether you are reading these guidelines or hearing me teach: the pulpit is not the place to show off your skills to anyone; it is the place from which you are privileged to serve the One who has called you by His grace.

Furthermore, nor is the pulpit the place to settle disputes or the place from which to provide entertainment, as many seem to think. You can share jokes to keep your listeners alert, but within the boundary of God's word. For example, I know of many preachers who will talk about people instead of preaching in the pulpit. This is wrong. Others take up most of their preaching time talking about themselves. They talk about who they are, and what they can do. There is nothing wrong in sharing your testimony when preaching or teaching, but be mindful; the preaching should not be about yourself, but about Jesus.

There are those who tell stories instead of preaching God's word and leave little time to preach. I have nothing against using stories and analogies, or even using proverbs in preaching or teaching. It may even be good to do that, and I sometimes do so myself. Even Jesus did it sometimes, for instance, when He used proverbs and physical objects to explain spiritual meanings. It becomes a problem when these are used excessively instead of preaching or teaching the word of God. The most common and probably worst mistake preachers can make is to misuse the opportunity presented to them. Instead of preaching, they show off, proudly telling people how much better they are than other preachers.

In 2 Timothy 4: 2 Paul instructed Timothy to 'Preach the word'. Preach the word! Be ready in season and out of season. Convince, rebuke, exhort, with all long suffering and teaching.' That is, whether the time is favourable or not, you must preach or teach the word. Do not be intimidated by anyone or any situation as you spread God's word. From the quotation above you can see that preaching or teaching must be done with conviction and offer your listeners or audience assurance. It must both offer rebuke and deliver exhortation: preaching and teaching must admonish people for their wrongdoings; reprimand, criticise or show disapproval of people's behaviour, if necessary. However, your message should also offer encouragement.

Further reading of 2 Timothy 4:3–5 offers a warning and provides encouragement:

> 'For the time will come when they will not endure sound doctrine, but according to their own desires, because they have itching ears, they will heap up for themselves teachers; and they will turn their ears away from the truth, and be turned aside to fables. But you be watchful in all things, endure afflictions, do the work of an evangelist, fulfil your ministry.'

Paul says 'time will come', and I believe that time is come here and now. This is the time when people will not put up with 'sound doctrine'. They will demand preachers and teachers to tell them what they want to hear, to suit their own desires. I once heard of a pastor who walked to the pulpit to preach but turned to prophesy because his members shouted to him 'Man of God, prophesy'! Know that you do not preach or teach what your listeners want to hear. Instead, you tell them what God wants you to tell them.

Preach Christ

The proclamation of any kind of message other than the Gospel, which alone is the true word of God revealed in the Bible and especially in Jesus Christ, is not preaching. This is to say that, discussion of politics, popular authors, or other current topics can rightfully be referred to as address but the message about the very truth of God's word through man to man is therefore may be called preaching

As preachers and teachers of God's word, Jesus Christ should be our theme. He must be the centre of everything we preach or teach. Christ must be the focus and the attention to which we direct our listeners. He is the only path to salvation, He sustains all life and only He offers eternal life. Christ is the object of our faith; it is in His name and by His power that we can be successful in our ministry of preaching and teaching. Remember what Paul said in Philippians 4.13: 'I can do all things through Christ who strengthens me'.

As I said previously, preachers must talk about Christ and not about themselves: I have witnessed many preachers and teachers who direct their audience or listeners' attention toward themselves instead of the real theme of their message—Christ our Lord.

Examples of preaching Christ

Acts 8:5: 'Then Philip went down to the city of Samaria and preached Christ to them.'

Acts 8:35: 'Then Philip opened his mouth, and beginning at this scripture, preached Jesus to him.'

Acts 9: 20: 'Immediately he preached Christ in the synagogues, that He is the Son of God.'

Acts 10: 36: 'The word which God sent to the children of Israel, preaching peace through Jesus Christ—He is Lord of all.'

Acts 17: 2–3: 'Then Paul, as his custom was, went in to them, and for three Sabbaths reasoned with them from the scriptures, explaining and demonstrating that Christ had to suffer and rise again from the dead, and saying, "This Jesus whom I preach to you is the Christ."'

1 Corinthians 1:22–24: 'For Jews request a sign, and Greeks seek after wisdom; but we preach Christ crucified, to the Jews a stumbling block and to the Greeks foolishness, but to those who are called, both Jews and Greeks, Christ the power of God and the wisdom of God.'

2 Corinthians 4:3–5: 'But even if our gospel is veiled, it is veiled to those who are perishing, whose minds the god of this age has blinded, who do not believe, lest the light of the gospel of the glory of Christ, who is the image of God, should shine on them. For we do not preach ourselves, but Christ Jesus the Lord, and ourselves your bond servants for Jesus' sake.'

In John 12:32–33 Jesus said, 'And I, when I am lifted up from the earth, will draw all people to myself.' The following verse says, 'This He said, signifying by what death He would die.' Within the context of these guidelines, when preachers and teachers of God's word preach and teach Christ, that is, when we lift Him up, He will through the power of the Holy Spirit convict people and bring them into repentance. I would like to make this important point clear: preaching or teaching about you yourself; someone or something else will not save anyone.

I remember inviting a preacher to come and talk at one of our church programmes, and knowing my congregation well, I was trying to persuade her to come on a day I knew we'd have good attendance. However, she said to me, 'Don't worry, the anointing will bring the people.' In fact, it happened just as she said. The anointing brought the people to the church even though those two days when she was minister were usually the days of least attendance.

When Christ is preached, when He is lifted up, He will always draw men to Him. Let Him be the centre of your message and you will always have success.

The true word will always provide better results

The undiluted word of God will subdue every opposition and bring every kingdom of darkness down. As told in Acts 17:6, the early Church turned the world upside down with God's word. But when they did not find the preachers, they dragged Jason and some brethren to the rulers of the city, crying out, 'These who have turned the world upside down have come here too.'

God will always back his word with power through the Holy Spirit, to bring conviction, repentance unto salvation, and freedom to the hearts of those who believe whenever the word is preached faithfully. In Romans 1:16–17 Paul pronounces, 'For I am not ashamed of the gospel of Christ, for it is the power of God unto salvation for everyone who believes, for the Jew first and also for the Greek. For in it the righteousness of God is revealed from faith to faith; as it is written, "The just shall live by faith."'

Other Important Points

In 1 Corinthians 1:18 we are told: 'For the message of the cross is foolishness to those who are perishing, but to us who are being saved it is the power of God.'

In Hebrews 4:12 we are told: 'For the word of God *is* living and powerful, and sharper than any two-edged sword, piercing even to the division of soul and spirit, and of joints and marrow, and is a discerner of the thoughts and intents of the heart.'

In Galatians 1: 9 Paul warns that it is wrong, and a curse to preach anything other than the gospel. 'As we have said before, so now I say again, if anyone preaches any other gospel to you than what you have received, let him be accursed.'

In Thessalonians 2:13 we are reminded that 'For this reason we also thank God without ceasing, because when you received the word of God which you heard from us, you welcomed *it* not *as* the word of men, but as it is in truth, the word of God, which also effectively works in you who believe.'

All the quotations cited above indicate that if you want better results through your message don't preach or teach about yourself or anything other than the word of God.

Teach or preach to please God not your fellow men

Do not try to please men but preach or teach to please God and you will benefit everyone. Many of Paul's letters were written to address particular situations, so we can also preach or teach to address particular experiences, but we must not do it in order to win people's approval. We must also not do it to condemn or insult someone; you must preach or teach for God and for the benefit of everyone.

Elitism

There is another point to stress about preaching or teaching. Some preaching favours people or a group of people over another. Some people preach or teach topics or messages influenced by other people. In other words, it is more about what people have told them to preach about instead of what God wants them to say. The point I am trying to make here is that people will cause you to say what you are not supposed to say, or say things at the wrong time or in the wrong place, and this is dangerous. I think it is time for preachers and teachers of God's word to do away with things of the flesh. Traditions, elitist messages and the need for peoples' approval or recommendations should completely vanish from our minds. Instead, we should preach or teach to honour God; a message that is directed or which is led by the Spirit. This is very important, no matter who may be offended in the process.

As a true minister of God, never preach or teach to please your listeners! Say what the Holy Spirit wants you to say and say it boldly. Do not get into the habit of false prophets who say always what the people want them to say. Do not be like some of the preachers and teachers today who also preach and teach to please their listeners. They do it to win the approval of men and this is against the word of God. The truth is that anyone who seeks to win the approval of men will not please God. In Galatians 1:10 Paul asks: 'Am I now trying to win the approval of men, or of God? Or am I trying to please men? If I were still trying to please men, I would not be a servant of Christ.'

In his first letter to the Thessalonians (1 Thessalonians 2:3–6) Paul wrote:

> 'For the appeal we make does not spring from error or impure motives, nor are we trying to trick you. On the contrary, we speak as men approved by God to be entrusted with the gospel. We are not trying to please men but God, who tests our hearts. You know we never used flattery, nor did we put on a mask to cover up greed—God is our witness. We were not looking for praise from men, not from

you or anyone else. As apostles of Christ we could have been a burden to you.'

Never dilute the scriptures to meet the crowd's approval or say what you know your listeners want to hear. A true preacher or teacher of God speaks the truth, regardless of what his audience wants to hear.

Personal testimony

I remind you and once again to the glory of God that because I preach the word, which is the truth, I also depend totally on the anointing of the Holy Spirit. As already mentioned, people often contact me after I have preached; some will be crying, others tell me they are shaking and cannot even stand on their feet. Once, someone told me that he had to stop driving because of the power of my message. He had been listening to my message while driving and because my message was so powerful he had to stop the car to recover. Many people have opened up to me about their intention to commit suicide; couples have confessed that they were ready to divorce, but reconsidered their decision because they heard me preach and they were touched.

The most wonderful part of my testimony is this: as I was writing these guidelines I had a phone call from a member of my church: 'Pastor,' she said, 'last Sunday as you were preaching, I could sense the power of God flowing through my body.' I shouted, 'Praise God!' I then told her exactly what I was doing, writing these guidelines, and told her that it is all by the power of the Holy Spirit. Never play down His assistance, for He knows the right thing to say at the right time. He knows what will meet your hearers' needs and touch their spirit. Preaching or teaching that does not bring conviction and draw listeners closer to God is of no benefit to those who hear you.

Causing offense

As a preacher and teacher of the word of God, I must tell you that there are times when you may offend some people. You may even receive insults because you are preaching or teaching the true word. Never be discouraged, for even Jesus faced this problem, as told in John 6:59–66.

I have experienced insults while preaching my message, 'Discover your transitional Period'. Another time, somebody confronted me and claimed that I was preaching about her. In every case, my joy is that my preaching has spoken directly to someone's life.

Pray for boldness

Preaching goes with boldness through the power of the Holy Spirit. No one can withstand you if you preach the true word of God. It is for this reason the apostles prayed for boldness when they were opposed and threatened so as not to preach about the name. Jesus. Acts 4:29 tell us: 'Now, Lord, look on their threats, and grant to Your servants that with all boldness they may speak Your word.'

Reflect on what you preach

There are two elements in preaching: **_man_** and **_message_** or **_personality_** and **_truth_**. Personality is important because the preacher's personality has much to do with the effectiveness of his message, which means, therefore, that personality does count for a lot when preaching.

Another way you can be backed up by the Holy Spirit in your preaching or teaching is to be a testimony of the message you preach or teach. Don't ask your listeners to consider only what you say and not what you do. You must reflect what you preach or teach, for it is not what you say but what you are and what you do that draws others to Christ. Some preachers cannot convince their listeners because they live a life contrary to what they preach. In 1 Corinthians 1:1 Paul tells his listeners in Corinth, 'Imitate me, just as I also imitate Christ.' All preachers and teachers must practise what they preach. They should be in the same position as Paul if they want to be effective preachers or teachers of God's word. Bear in mind that some of your listeners may know you personally and could judge you if you lead a life that is contrary to the one you preach. In 1 Corinthians 9:27 Paul tells the Corinthians that he tries to live up to the standards he preaches, he said: 'No, I beat my body and make it my slave so that after I have preached to others, I myself will not be disqualified for the prize.'

It is very important to practise what you preach because preachers, and in the current context teachers too, are representatives of God as declared by the prophet in Malachi 2:7–9:

> "'For the lips of a priest ought to preserve knowledge, and from his mouth men should seek instruction—because he is the messenger Lord Almighty. But you have turned from the way and by your teaching have caused many to stumble; you have violated the covenant with Levi" said the Lord Almighty. "So I have caused you to be despised and humiliated before all the people, because you have not followed my ways but have shown partiality in matters of the law.'"

Again the writer of the book of Hebrews advises his readers to imitate the faith of those who preach and teach them the word. He said: Remember your leaders, who spoke the word of God to you. Consider the outcome of their way of life and imitate their faith. Hebrews 13:7

Never be disqualified by what you preach or teach as it will not help you to become an effective guardian of God's word. One way for people to judge the effectiveness of your message is to see the word at work in the life of their preacher or teacher. I have said this many times before; listeners will benefit and prosper and may even go to heaven because of a preacher or teacher's message. Yet, the preacher or teacher themselves will not benefit—some may even go to hell—because they did not live by what they were preaching or teaching. My final question to you is: Is your life as a preacher or teacher of God's word well emulated by your listeners? If your answer is no, please change.

Awareness

The preacher and teacher of God's word must not only be aware of his personal call to ministry but must also be convinced of the validity of the message he carries. He must be persuaded of the love and wrath of the Lord he preaches or teaches before he can persuade others (2 Corinthians 5:1)

As I said earlier in this book of guidance, preachers and teachers must reflect on what they teach or preach because they will be judged according to what they say. James (James 3:1) advised his readers about this, 'My brethren, let not many of you become teachers, knowing that we shall receive a stricter judgement.'

If you compare James 3:1 with Ephesians 4:11, which says, 'And He Himself gave some to be apostles, some prophets, some evangelists, and some pastors and teachers.' it becomes clear that some people are called to teach. If you are one of those who are called, as James says, you must be mindful because you will receive a stricter judgement. Therefore be sure you practise what you preach. Don't be one of those who say, 'Listen to me but don't look at me.' This is one of the reasons, nowadays, why people don't respond to preaching and teaching because they see preachers living contrary to their own message.

Your message reveals who you are

Your listeners will know if you are genuine by the way you live your life. Jesus tells his listeners how to identify false prophets as told in Matthew 7: 15–20:

> 'Beware of false prophets, who come to you in sheep's clothing, but inwardly they are ravenous

wolves. You will know them by their fruits. Do men gather grapes from thorn bushes or figs from thistles? Even so, every good tree bears good fruit, but a bad tree bears bad fruit. A good tree cannot bear bad fruit, nor *can* a bad tree bear good fruit. Every tree that does not bear good fruit is cut down and thrown into the fire. Therefore by their fruits you will know them.'

As recorded in John 7:16–18, in his teaching, Jesus indicated that preachers and teachers must always agree with, and not contradict, the Bible. The focus of the preaching or teaching should always shine a light on God and His will and never put a spotlight on the preacher. Jesus said:

'My doctrine is not Mine, but His who sent Me. If anyone wants to do His will, he shall know concerning the doctrine, whether it is from God or whether I speak on My own authority. He who speaks from himself seeks his own glory; but He who seeks the glory of the One who sent Him is true, and no unrighteousness is in Him.'

What is meant by this is that if you place emphasis on yourself, and also say things which are contrary to the Bible, you will be exposed. As John so rightly said, 'He must increase, but I must decrease.'

Conclusion

Therefore, always remember that to be effective in your preaching and teaching, you must first be taught; you must always be led by the Holy Spirit. You must be prayerful, read and study the word exhaustively. Spend time in preparation and familiarise yourself with the message you want to convey. Your desire to convey that message must be habitual despite the possibility of opposition to your preaching or teaching. Some people will not accept your message, but will instead choose to be offended, and will not repent their life, contrary to God's word. They will not see it as the Lord speaking through you. Also be aware that someone might even attack you, either physically or spiritually, and accuse you of talking against them. Don't worry, but rejoice that your message had spoken to someone.

You must be a hard worker and a good listener too, hear what other preachers and teachers have to say, in order that you shall learn from them. This will help you become a better preacher or teacher. However, be careful not to try to be like these people, be mindful to be yourself. Bear in mind that it takes time and effort to become a good and experienced preacher or teacher. Also, that sometimes after you preach or teach you may feel that you did not do well. Do not worry. Do not be disappointed, such things do happen sometimes. Providing that it is not due to improper preparation on the part of the preacher or teacher, put the experience behind you. I know that many people see me as a successful pastor, preacher and teacher of God's word. I would like to thank God for that, but I should also like to stress that I did not become an accomplished preacher or teacher overnight. It was through the grace of God given to me and also through hard work. I study hard, to show myself approved unto God, and spend time seeking God for what to preach and teach. One day, my little daughter asked me, 'Daddy, why are you always on the computer?' 'I am studying of course,' I told her.

Always remember that you are a preacher or teacher of God's word. The pulpit is not a right it is a privilege: it is a privilege to spread God's word and nothing else. Respect the pulpit and use it only for God's purpose, not for any personal battle, such as insulting others or talking about a dispute between you and someone else. It is not a place to prove yourself to anybody it is a place to serve your master.

Preach the word and preach Christ and you will always have good results.

Conclusion

I hope you have been blessed with these guidelines and that it will help you improve your teaching and preaching skills.

God richly bless you.

Other Publications by Pastor David Amoah

Lead Us Not Into Temptation

Be Ye Transformed

Your Future Is In your Hands

The Power For Your Zero Hour

Stay Connected To Christ

www.ingramcontent.com/pod-product-compliance
Lightning Source LLC
Chambersburg PA
CBHW071027080526
44587CB00015B/2533